PHILLIP HUGHES

AUSTRALIAN CRICKETER

MR VIVEK KUMAR PANDEY SHAMBHUNATH

ISBN 979-888555636-1

Disclaimer : During Writing This Book No character & No religious , No Relation Members Are Harmed. It's Only For Study & Entertainment Purpose. Do Not Take Seriously. Short Biopic Written In This Book Written By Mr Vivek Kumar Pandey.

Contents

Foreword

Short biography of Phillip Hughes and about life.During writing this book no character & no religious are harmed written by Mr Vivek Kumar Pandey. winner youngest writer award 1st rank in india 2020.He is only one writer can publish 770+ own book that was greatest successfull in his life.This All Credit Goes To My Super Hero Daddy.

Preface

Author biography in English :MY NAME IS VIVEK KUMAR PANDEY . I WAS BORN IN 30 SEP 2002,I AM FROM SURAT GUJARAT INDIA.MY DREAM WAS TO BE GOOD WRITERS ,MY FAMILY SUPPORTED ME TO SUCCESSFUL AND I CAN DO IT MY SELF.How do I write? That is a question, I believe, that can be honestly answered by me."CELEBRATING YOUNGEST WRITER AWARD WINNER IN GUJARAT 1ST RANK" MR PANDEY JI . I may think I did a good job writing something . The reader is the one who decides the quality of my writing. I do find writing to be natural to me and therefore find it to be a real challenge. My trick as a challenged writer is to do the best I can and know that I am happy with the final outcome. It may take a while to do my best and there may be quite a few problems I run into along the way.

I am not a greedy person those who are thinking about me and my self I never tried it anyone people suffering from sadness ,I trying to get promoted people suffering from happiness and joy in your Life Time. Now in current situation in India and also world people are unemployed and have no many but our indian governor help to people to get free food from ration card , i also take part in leadership team ,i am Motivational speaker , Film script writer. There was my two dream firstly writer and secondly actor & also my own film is upcoming soon i done almost completely completed script for my film .I AM GOING TO SAY WORD OF HEART TOUCH OUT PLEASE READ IT" , firstly i thanks my father he supports me in this field they always getting inspired me by own his words and behavior ,they always said that he was a biggest person in the world in future and also they purchase fruit and chocolate for me in anytime & anyway , firstly my father buy him then call me Vivek you want a chocolate i will say yes papa but how many tell me ,papa: you tell me how much i buy him i told 1 or 2 chocolate but my father purchase whole the boxes of chocolate and they get suprised me. MY FATHER WAS BORN IN " 20 SEPTEMBER" 1971 IN INDIA.

1) MY FATHER FAVORITE CLOTHES IS KURTA PAIJMA AND ALSO STYLES SHOE

2) FAVORITE SINGER IS KISHORE DA

3) FAVORITE STATE GUJARAT AND KOLKATA , HIS VILLAGE IN BIHAR

4) FAVORITE COLOR BLACK AND WHITE

THEY ALSO LOVE cricket like IPL and one day t-20 .they also like watching a News daily and heard the song daily ,they also interested in tik tok video but in current time tik tok is banned in india but also few videos are in you tube. In lockdown time my family and me very enjoy day daily. my father play daily ludo with his sister and son, daughter.they always loved tea and coffee anytime call me "। वविके थोडा़ चाय बनाओना वविके तमु्हारे हाथ का चाय अच्छा लगता है". I make it tea for my father but some reason after the April to june they are suffering from fever and cough , weakness on 6 June 2020 my father death. they not told me say bye bye his life. After death of 6 June on 10 june my mom and dad anniversary.but my father is Best in the world they can do anything for me please take care of father and respect it of your parents.

CHAPTER ONE

Phillip Hughes

- *Phillip Hughes*
- *WE REALLY MISS THIS HERO (PHILLIPS HUGHES)*

1. Disclaimer : During Writing This Book No character & No religious , No Relation Members Are Harmed. It's Only For Study & Entertainment Purpose. Do Not Take Seriously. Short Biopic Written In This Book Written By Mr Vivek Kumar Pandey.

Phillip Joel Hughes (30 November 1988 – 27 November 2014) was an Australian Test and One Day International (ODI) cricketer who played domestic cricket for South Australia and Worcestershire. He was a left-handed opening batsman who played for two seasons with New South Wales before making his Test debut in 2009 at the age of 20. He made his One Day International Debut in 2013.

Hughes scored his first Test century in March 2009, aged 20, in his second Test match for Australia, opening the batting and hitting 115 in the first innings against South Africa in Durban. This made Hughes Australia's youngest Test centurion since Doug Walters in 1965. In the second innings of the same match, Hughes scored 160, becoming the youngest cricketer in history to score centuries in both innings of a Test match (Australia won the match by 175 runs). On 11 January 2013, he became the first Australian batsman in the history of ODI cricket to score a century on debut, a feat which he achieved against Sri Lanka in Melbourne.

On 25 November 2014, Hughes was hit in the neck by a bouncer, during a Sheffield Shield match at the Sydney Cricket Ground, causing a vertebral artery dissection that led to a subarachnoid hemorrhage. The Australian team doctor, Peter Brukner, noted that only 100 such cases had ever been reported, with "only one case reported as a result of a cricket ball". Hughes was taken to St Vincent's Hospital in Sydney, where he underwent surgery, was placed into an induced coma and was in intensive care in a critical condition.He never regained consciousness, and died on 27 November, three days before his 26th birthday.

- *Phillip Hughes life and junior career*

Hughes was born in Macksville, New South Wales, to father Greg, a banana farmer, and Italian mother, Virginia. Hughes was also a talented rugby league footballer who once played alongside former Australia international Greg Inglis. He played his junior cricket for Macksville RSL Cricket Club, where he excelled so quickly that he was playing A-Grade at the age of 12 and in Representative Cricket he scored a century. At the age of 17, Hughes moved from Macksville to Sydney to play for Western Suburbs District Cricket Club in Sydney Grade Cricket while he attended Homebush Boys High. He scored 141* on his grade debut and enjoyed a solid 2006–07 season, scoring 752 runs at an average of 35.81, with a highest score of 142*. He represented Australia at the 2008 ICC Under-19 Cricket World Cup. He was coached at Triforce Sports Cricket Centre in Mortlake.

- *Phillip Hughes First-class career*

After scoring runs prolifically for New South Wales youth teams and Western Suburbs in Grade Cricket, Hughes was handed a rookie contract by New South Wales for the 2007–08 season. After scores of 51 and 137 for the New South Wales Second XI against Victoria's Second XI,He was rewarded with a call-up by Blues selectors to make his first-class debut. He played his first senior game against Tasmania on 20 November 2007 at the Sydney Cricket Ground. At 18 years and 355 days, Hughes was the youngest New South Wales debutant since Michael Clarke in 1999. In a comfortable victory for New South Wales, Hughes opened the batting and got his career off to a solid start, scoring a fluent 51 and taking 2 catches.

- Hughes had an outstanding debut season for New South Wales, playing seven matches and scoring 559 runs at an average of 62.11 with one century and six 50s. The highlight of Hughes' excellent season came in New South Wales' Pura Cup final victory over Victoria. He scored

116 off 175 balls in the Blues' second innings to help put his team in a commanding position. At 19 years of age, this innings made him the youngest-ever player to score a century in a Sheffield Shield final. Hughes was rewarded for his achievements by winning the New South Wales Rising Star Award and earning an upgrade to a full state contract for the 2008–09 season.

Hughes was signed by Middlesex on a short-term contract, as cover for Murali Kartik, for the beginning of the 2009 English cricket season. He was available for the first six weeks of the season and played in three County Championship matches, all eight of Middlesex's Friends Provident Trophy group matches and the first few matches in the Panthers' defence of the Twenty20 Cup.

In most other years, a contract for the opening six weeks of the season would involve playing four to six championship matches, some but not all FPT matches and no Twenty20, but the scheduling for 2009 had to accommodate ICC World Twenty20 and the eventually-cancelled Stanford Super Series. Despite Hughes holding an Italian passport by virtue of his Italian mother, Middlesex resisted signing him up as a Kolpak player and instead signed him as a foreign player. He enjoyed strong success in England, scoring 574 runs in his three first-class matches, including three hundreds, at an average of 143.50. Of his time at Middlesex, Hughes commented.

I thoroughly enjoyed it and the preparation has been great. The big thing that came out of it was that I played at three Test grounds I'm going to be playing on and got to experience them before this big series coming up. Lord's was my home ground there for Middlesex and I played at The Oval as well and Edgbaston. It couldn't have really worked out any better. The big thing was just going over there to experience the whole different culture really, the weather, the wickets and the bowlers as well."

Hughes hit consecutive hundreds at the end of the 2010/11 season to earn the praise of Australian chairman of selectors Andrew Hilditch. In his last two first-class matches for New South Wales in the 2010/11 season he scored 54, 115, 138 and 93. Australia's chairman of selectors, Andrew Hilditch, said "I was thrilled for Phil, I think he turned the corner the last game. I spent a bit of time with him before the last Shield game and he seemed to be in a really good place. Having had a tough season, to emerge like he has is a credit to him."

- *Phillip Hughes List A career*

Less than a week after his debut in first-class cricket, on 28 November 2007, Hughes made his List A debut against Victoria at the Melbourne Cricket Ground. While he was not originally scheduled to play the match, sickness to Australian opening batsman Phil Jaques handed him the spot. Just as he did in his first-class debut, Hughes passed 50 but was eventually dismissed for 68, top scoring for New South Wales in a "controlled" display.

After New South Wales' wicket-keeper Brad Haddin was struck in the head by a top edge, Hughes took on the keeping duties for nine overs. On 17 May 2009, Hughes made his first limited overs century, scoring 119 for Middlesex against Warwickshire. On 29 July 2014, he made a double century (202 not out from 151 balls) in a match with South Africa A in Darwin.

- *Phillip Hughes Australian international career*

Ducking to a short ball that, according to critics, caused him problems in England.After consistently making runs at domestic level, Hughes was called up to replace Matthew Hayden on Australia's tour of South Africa in February and March 2009. He was selected to make his debut in the first Test match starting on 26 February 2009 at the New Wanderers Stadium in Johannesburg after making 53, then retiring, in Australia's tour match against the South African Board President's XI. He was dismissed for a duck in his first Test innings by Dale Steyn off just the fourth ball of the match, however he went on to top-score with 75 in the second innings, including 11 fours and a six.

Hughes hit his maiden Test century in the first innings of the second Test at the Sahara Stadium, Kingsmead, Durban, on 6 March 2009, before adding another hundred in the second Innings. In doing so, at the age of 20 years and 96 days, he became both the youngest Australian since Doug Walters to score a Test century and the youngest player from any country to score a century in both innings of a Test match.

- *Hughes at Northampton in July 2009*

During the 2009 Ashes campaign, Hughes‘ unorthodox technique was exploited by fast bowlers, who targeted his upper body and avoided bowling wide outside off stump, restricting his opportunities to play shots through the offside, most notably the cut shot. He was dropped from the team for the third Edgbaston Test in favour of Shane Watson, who opened the batting in his place and provided the Australians with an extra bowling option. Upon his return from South Africa, the Phillip Hughes Award, to be given annually to a promising young cricketer from the local district, was announced in his home town of Macksville. He was awarded the Bradman Young Cricketer of the Year at the Allan Border Medal ceremony by the CA in 2009.

- Hughes was a fringe player for the next year or so, playing some Tests to cover for other injured batsmen. He played two home Tests against Pakistan in this capacity, covering for the injured Ricky Ponting in the Boxing Day Test, then Simon Katich in the New Year's Test. He was then called up to the Test squad for the tour of New Zealand in March 2010 to replace Shane Watson in the first Test; he scored a rapid 86 from 75 balls in a small fourth-innings run chase in this Test.

Hughes was dropped from the 2010–11 Ashes squad, but was called up for the Third Test as a replacement for the injured Simon Katich. He was a regular in the Australian team for the following year, playing in the last three Ashes tests, tours of Sri Lanka and South Africa and then a home series against New Zealand, but his spot came under pressure due to his inconsistency during that time. He achieved two big scores (126 in Colombo and 88 in Johannesburg), but his next-highest score was only 36, and he consistently fell to catches at slip and gully. He was heavily criticised for his performance in the two-Test series against New Zealand, in which he managed only 41 runs at 10.25, and was dismissed exactly the same way in all four innings: caught at slip by Martin Guptill from the bowling of Chris Martin. He was dropped from the Australian team following the series.

- In a stint for Worcestershire in the English County Cricket competition, Hughes made adjustments to his much maligned technique resulting in a more expansive range of strokes with more emphasis on legside play. Upon return to Australia, Hughes left his home state of New South Wales, moving to South Australia. This resulted in a strong return of runs in first-class cricket in the Sheffield Shield and one day cricket in the Ryobi Cup. These returns earned Hughes a recall to the Australian

Test team to face Sri Lanka in Hobart following the retirement of Ricky Ponting in December 2012. He made an impressive first inning 86 batting at number 3.

After almost a year away from the Test arena, Hughes found himself back in the Test side for the series against Sri Lanka in lieu of the retiring Ricky Ponting, occupying the number 3 position over Watson. Immediately he made an impact, scoring a solid 86 in the first Test match at Hobart, with a new-found confidence and tighter technique that had eluded him 12 months prior. He made two half centuries during his comeback scoring 233 runs at 46.60 in what was the most successful stint at the number 3 spot that the Australians had seen for some time.

Hughes was set to receive a $1 million contract with Cricket Australia and be selected in Australia's ODI and T20 international squads in the wake of Michael Hussey's international retirement at the end of the 2012/13 Australia summer. Hughes' selection in the Australian ODI squad was confirmed on 6 January 2013. National selection boss John Inverarity noted that players such as Hughes were included with an eye to the 2015 World Cup, suggesting that he was viewed as a long-term player for Australia in all three forms of the game.

Hughes made his mark with a solid 112 (from 129 balls) in his ODI debut, becoming the first Australian to reach a century on debut. He opened the innings with Aaron Finch at Melbourne, and added a 140-run 3rd wicket partnership with captain George Bailey, before being dismissed by Lasith Malinga. Hughes scored his 2nd match-winning ODI century with 138 (n.o) off 154 balls in the fifth ODI of the same series.

Following his successful summer season in Australia in 2012/2013, Hughes was selected to play in the Test series in India, but he struggled, scoring 147 runs in eight innings and averaging only 18.37. He played the first two Tests of the 2013 Ashes, and shared a world record tenth wicket partnership of 163 runs with debutant Ashton Agar in the first innings at Trent Bridge, but was dropped for the third test.Hughes did not play another Test for Australia, but played in ODI series in India in October 2013, in Zimbabwe (against both Zimbabwe and South Africa) in September 2014, and against Pakistan in the UAE in October 2014. Hughes made his only Twenty20 International appearance for Australia against Pakistan in the United Arab Emirates on 5 October 2014.

- *Phillip Hughes Awards*

1. New South Wales Rising Star Award: 2008
2. Bradman Young Cricketer of the Year: 2009
3. Sheffield Shield Player of the Year: 2008/09
4. Domestic Player of the Year: 2012/13

- *Phillip Hughes Personal life*

A year before his death, Hughes bought a 90-hectare (220-acre) property in Macksville, with 70 Angus cattle.He was a close friend of teammates Michael Clarke and David Warner, as well as boxer Anthony Mundine. He grew up with fellow Macksville local and former rugby league footballer; Greg Inglis.

- *Phillip Hughes Death*

During a session of the Sheffield Shield match between South Australia and New South Wales at the Sydney Cricket Ground on 25 November 2014, Hughes, batting on 63 runs, was struck in the neck by the ball after missing an attempted hook shot to a bouncer from New South Wales bowler Sean Abbott. Hughes was wearing a helmet, but the ball struck an unprotected area just below his left ear. He collapsed before receiving mouth-to-mouth resuscitation and was subsequently taken to St Vincent's Hospital, Sydney, where he underwent surgery and was placed into an induced coma. Hughes' injury was a rare but described type of sport-related blunt-force cerebrovascular injury called a vertebral artery dissection which led to subarachnoid haemorrhage.

The match was immediately abandoned. The other two Shield games that were being played elsewhere in Australia—Brisbane and Melbourne—were abandoned at the end of the day, with Cricket Australia stating that "Given how players across the country are feeling right now, it's just not the day to be playing cricket."

On the morning of 27 November 2014, Hughes died from his injuries, three days before his 26th birthday. Australian cricket captain Michael Clarke read a statement on behalf of Hughes' family.In May 2015, Cricket Australia announced that an independent review would be undertaken into Hughes' death.

As a result of Hughes' death, calls were made for improvements to the cricket helmet, and this has resulted in new designs which have additional guards fitted to the rear of the helmet. However, an independent review released by Cricket Australia states that "The now mandated British Standard helmet would have offered no protection where he was struck. There is limited scientific evidence that current neck guards will prevent a similar tragedy and they must be properly evaluated before they are mandated.

"After the review was completed in 2016, it was concluded that the incident was purely accidental, and any changes made to improve safety during the review period, such as mandatory helmets for wicketkeepers, close-in fielders, and batsmen facing fast or medium pace bowling (even during net sessions) would not have prevented the accident. Also, for all Cricket Australia-sanctioned matches, defibrillators must be available at all grounds.

- *Phillip Hughes Inquest*

A coronial inquest into Hughes‘ death began on 10 October 2016. The final result of investigation was that death of Hughes was a tragic accident arising from a minuscule misjudgement from the batsman and no players or umpires were at fault.

- *Phillip Hughes Tributes*

Many tributes were paid to Hughes within and outside the world of cricket, particularly over the rest of the 2014–15 summer season. Play on the second day of the third Test between Pakistan and New Zealand in the United Arab Emirates was suspended, due to its scheduled start occurring not long after Hughes' death. The match was extended by an extra day. The second ODI between Sri Lanka and England, played on 29 November, went ahead with the teams paying tribute to Hughes. People from around the world posted photos of their bats on social media to pay tribute to Hughes.

Hughes‘ funeral was held on 3 December 2014 at Macksville High School, in a Catholic ceremony. The eulogy was given by Hughes' cousin, Nino Ramunno, with speeches also given by Hughes‘ siblings Jason and Megan; Michael Clarke and James Sutherland. Clarke, Aaron Finch and Tom Cooper were among the pallbearers. The service was attended by around one thousand people, including many national and sporting dignitaries as well as Australian Prime Minister Tony Abbott. Thousands of people followed the service at venues in Macksville and around the country. Representatives from the Indian team touring the country also attended.

The first two matches of that series between Australia and India, to have been held in early December, were rescheduled to provide an additional five days of mourning. Hughes was named and listed as "the 13th man" for the first Test, and his test cap number 408 was sewn under the badge of all Australian players and painted on the field, and there were 63 seconds of applause before the start of the match.

During the first Test, David Warner and Steve Smith both raised their bats in commemoration of Phillip Hughes when they passed 63 not out, and when Australia reached 408 runs, the match temporarily stopped as the crowd recognised the occasion. When Warner passed 63 in the fourth Test at the SCG, he kissed the ground near to the place where Hughes was fatally injured. Clarke continued to wear a black armband with Hughes's initials on it through to the final of the 2015 Cricket World Cup and dedicated their victory at the MCG over co-host New Zealand to Hughes after Australia reclaimed the World Cup.

Hughes' One-Day International shirt number, 64, was retired in his memory. The scorecard of Hughes' final innings was formally amended to show him being 63 not out, instead of retired hurt. A 63-over tribute match (31½ overs per team) featuring some Australians was played in Nepal on 11 April 2015. During the men's trials for the 2015 Boat Race contested by Oxford and Cambridge, the senior men's trial boats for the Cambridge team were called 63 and Not Out in honour of Hughes.

Sydney rapper Urthboy released "Nambucca Boy" as a tribute to Hughes. Matthew Wade also has a likeness of Hughes tattooed on his right forearm.

In the first home Ashes series since Hughes' passing, Australia decided to extend play to the 5th day on the First Ashes Test in 2017, which coincided with the third anniversary of his passing, with David Warner looking skyward as he scored past 63*, with the Barmy Army also sang a parody as a tribute to Hughes to the tune of "Walking in a Winter Wonderland". Australia won the first test at The Gabba, Brisbane by 10 wickets.

On 16 December 2017, it was announced by the NSW Roads Minister, Melinda Pavey, that the new bridge on the Pacific Highway over the Nambucca River near his rural NSW hometown of Macksville is to be named after Hughes.

CHAPTER TWO

Australia national cricket team

- Australia national cricket team

The Australia men's national cricket team represents Australia in men's international cricket. As the joint oldest team in Test cricket history, playing in the first ever Test match in 1877, the team also plays One-Day International (ODI) and Twenty20 International (T20I) cricket, participating in both the first ODI, against England in the 1970–71 season and the first T20I, against New Zealand in the 2004–05 season, winning both games. The team draws its players from teams playing in the Australian domestic competitions – the Sheffield Shield, the Australian domestic limited-overs cricket tournament and the Big Bash League.

The national team has played 837 Test matches, winning 397, losing 226, drawing 212 and tying 2. As of January 2021, Australia is ranked third in the ICC Test Championship on 113 rating points. Australia is the most successful team in Test cricket history, in terms of overall wins, win-loss ratio and wins percentage.

Test rivalries include The Ashes (with England), The Border-Gavaskar Trophy (with India), the Frank Worrell Trophy (with the West Indies), the Trans-Tasman Trophy (with New Zealand), and with South Africa.

The team has played 958 ODI matches, winning 581, losing 334, tying 9 and with 34 ending in a no-result. As of January 2021, Australia is ranked fourth in the ICC ODI Championship on 111 rating points, though have been ranked first for 141 of 185 months since its introduction in 2002.

Australia is the most successful team in ODI cricket history, winning more than 60 per cent of their matches, with a record seven World Cup final appearances (1975, 1987, 1996, 1999, 2003, 2007 and 2015) and have won the World Cup a record five times: 1987, 1999, 2003, 2007 and 2015. Australia is the first (and only) team to appear in four consecutive World Cup finals (1996, 1999, 2003 and 2007), surpassing the old record of three consecutive World Cup appearances by the West Indies (1975, 1979 and 1983) and the first and only team to win 3 consecutive World Cups (1999, 2003 and 2007). The team was undefeated in 34 consecutive World Cup matches until the 2011 Cricket World Cup where Pakistan beat them by 4 wickets in the Group stage.

It is also the second team to win a World Cup (2015) on home soil, after India (2011). Australia have also won the ICC Champions Trophy twice (2006 and 2009) making them the first and the only team to become back to back winners in the Champions Trophy tournaments. As of 2021, Australia is the only team to win five Cricket World Cups; no other team has won more than two.

The national team has played 153 Twenty20 International matches, winning 79, losing 69, tying 2 and with 3 ending in a no-result. As of November 2021, Australia is ranked sixth in the ICC T20I Championship on 246 rating points. Australia are the reigning ICC Men's T20 World Cup champions, defeating New Zealand in the 2021 final to claim their first T20 World Cup title.

On 12 January 2019, Australia won the first ODI against India at the Sydney Cricket Ground by 34 runs, to record their 1,000th win in international cricket.

- Australian cricket from 1876–77 to 1890

The Australian team that toured England in 1878

The Australian cricket team participated in the first Test match at the MCG in 1877, defeating an English team by 45 runs, with Charles Bannerman making the first Test century, a score of 165 retired hurt.Test cricket, which only occurred between Australia and England at the time, was limited by the long distance between the two countries, which would take several months by sea. Despite Australia's much smaller population, the team was very competitive in early games, producing stars such as Jack Blackham, Billy Murdoch, Fred "The Demon" Spofforth, George Bonnor, Percy McDonnell, George Giffen and Charles "The Terror" Turner. Most cricketers at the time were either from New South Wales or Victoria, with the notable exception of George Giffen, the star South Australian all-rounder.

A highlight of Australia's early history was the 1882 Test match against England at The Oval. In this match, Fred Spofforth took 7/44 in the game's fourth innings to save the match by preventing England from making their 85-run target. After this match The Sporting Times, a major newspaper in London at the time, printed a mock obituary in which the death of English cricket was proclaimed and the announcement made that "the body was cremated and the ashes taken to Australia." This was the start of the famous Ashes series in which Australia and England play a series of Test matches to decide the holder of the Ashes. To this day, the contest is one of the fiercest rivalries in sport.

- Golden age

History of Australian cricket from 1890–91 to 1900 and History of Australian cricket from 1900–01 to 1918

The so-called 'Golden Age' of Australian Test cricket occurred around the end of the 19th century and the beginning of the 20th century, with the team under the captaincy of Joe Darling, Monty Noble and Clem Hill winning eight of ten tours. It is considered to have lasted from the 1897–98 English tour of Australia and the 1910–11 South African tour of Australia. Outstanding batsmen such as Joe Darling, Clem Hill, Reggie Duff, Syd Gregory, Warren Bardsley and Victor Trumper, brilliant all-rounders including Monty Noble, George Giffen, Harry Trott and Warwick Armstrong and excellent bowlers including Ernie Jones, Hugh Trumble, Tibby Cotter, Bill Howell, Jack Saunders and Bill Whitty, all helped Australia to become the dominant cricketing nation for most of this period.

Victor Trumper became one of Australia's first sporting heroes, and was widely considered Australia's greatest batsman before Bradman and one of the most popular players. He played a record (at the time) number of Tests at 49 and scored 3163 (another record) runs at a high for the time average of 39.04. His early death in 1915 at the age of 37 from kidney disease caused national mourning. The Wisden Cricketers' Almanack, in its obituary for him, called him Australia's greatest batsman: "Of all the great Australian batsmen Victor Trumper was by general consent the best and most brilliant."

The years leading up to the start of World War I were marred by conflict between the players, led by Clem Hill, Victor Trumper and Frank Laver, the Australian Board of Control for International Cricket, led by Peter McAlister, who was attempting to gain more control of tours from the players. This led to six leading players (the so-called "Big Six") walking out on the 1912 Triangular Tournament in England, with Australia fielding what was generally considered a second-rate side. This was the last series before the war, and no more cricket was played by Australia for eight years, with Tibby Cotter being killed in Palestine during the war.

- Australian cricket from 1918–19 to 1930

Test cricket resumed in the 1920/21 season in Australia with a touring English team, captained by Johnny Douglas losing all five Tests to Australia, captained by the "Big Ship" Warwick Armstrong. Several players from before the war, including Warwick Armstrong, Charlie Macartney, Charles Kelleway, Warren Bardsley and the wicket-keeper Sammy Carter, were instrumental in the team's success, as well as new players Herbie Collins, Jack Ryder, Bert Oldfield, the spinner Arthur Mailey and the so-called "twin destroyers" Jack Gregory and Ted McDonald. The team continued its success on the 1921 tour of England, winning three out of the five Tests in Warwick Armstrong's last series. The side was, on the whole, inconsistent in the latter half of the 1920s, losing its first home Ashes series since the 1911–12 season in 1928–29.

- Australian cricket from 1930–31 to 1945

The 1930 tour of England heralded a new age of success for the Australian team. The team, led by Bill Woodfull – the "Great Un-bowlable" – featured legends of the game including Bill Ponsford, Stan McCabe, Clarrie Grimmett and the young pair of Archie Jackson and Don Bradman. Bradman was the outstanding batsman of the series, scoring a record 974 runs, including one century, two double centuries and one triple century, a massive score of 334 at Leeds which including 309 runs in a day. Jackson died of tuberculosis at the age of 23 three years later, after playing eight Tests. The team was widely considered unstoppable, winning nine of its next ten Tests.

The 1932–33 England tour of Australia is considered one of the most infamous episodes of cricket, due to the England team's use of bodyline, where captain Douglas Jardine instructed his bowlers Bill Voce and Harold Larwood to bowl fast, short-pitched deliveries aimed at the bodies of the Australian batsmen. The tactic, although effective, was widely considered by Australian crowds as vicious and unsporting. Injuries to Bill Woodfull, who was struck over the heart, and Bert Oldfield, who received a fractured skull (although from a non-bodyline ball), exacerbated the situation, almost causing a full-scale riot from the 50 000 fans at the Adelaide Oval for the third Test.

The conflict almost escalated into a diplomatic incident between the two countries, as leading Australian political figures, including the Governor of South Australia, Alexander Hore-Ruthven, protested to their English counterparts. The series ended in a 4–1 win for England but the bodyline tactics used were banned the year after.

The Australian team put the result of this series behind them, winning their next tour of England in 1934. The team was led by Bill Woodfull on his final tour and was notably dominated by Ponsford and Bradman, who twice put on partnerships of over 380 runs, with Bradman once again scoring a triple-century at Leeds. The bowling was dominated by the spin pair of Bill O'Reilly and Clarrie Grimmett, who took 53 wickets between them, with O'Reilly twice taking seven-wicket hauls.

Sir Donald Bradman is widely considered the greatest batsman of all time. He dominated the sport from 1930 until his retirement in 1948, setting new records for the highest score in a Test innings (334 vs England at Headingley in 1930), the most runs (6996), the most centuries (29), the most double centuries and the highest Test and first-class batting averages. His record for the highest Test batting average – 99.94 – has never been beaten. It is almost 40 runs per innings above the next highest average. He would have finished with an average of over 100 runs per innings if he had not been dismissed for a duck in his last Test. He was knighted in 1949 for services to cricket. He is generally considered one of Australia's greatest sporting heroes.

Test cricket was again interrupted by war, with the last Test series in 1938 made notable by Len Hutton scoring a world record 364 for England, with Chuck Fleetwood-Smith conceding 298 runs in England's world record total of 7/903. Ross Gregory, a notable young batsman who played two Tests before the war, was killed in the war.

- Australian cricket from 1945–46 to 1960

The team continued its success after the end of the Second World War, with the first Test (also Australia's first against New Zealand) being played in the 1945–46 season against New Zealand. Australia was by far the most successful team of the 1940s, being undefeated throughout the decade, winning two Ashes series against England and its first Test series against India. The team capitalised on its ageing stars Bradman, Sid Barnes, Bill Brown and Lindsay Hassett while new talent, including Ian Johnson, Don Tallon, Arthur Morris, Neil Harvey, Bill Johnston and the fast bowling pair of Ray Lindwall and Keith Miller, who all made their debut in the latter half of the 1940s, and were to form the basis of the team for a good part of the next decade. The team that Don Bradman led to England in 1948 gained the moniker The Invincibles, after going through the tour without losing a single game.

Of 31 first-class games played during the tour, they won 23 and drew 8, including winning the five-match Test series 4–0, with one draw. The tour was particularly notable for the fourth Test of the series, in which Australia won by seven wickets chasing a target of 404, setting a new record for the highest run chase in Test cricket, with Arthur Morris and Bradman both scoring centuries, as well as for the final Test in the series, Bradman's last, where he finished with a duck in his last innings after needing only four runs to secure a career average of 100.

Australia was less successful in the 1950s, losing three consecutive Ashes series to England, including a horrendous 1956 Tour of England, where the 'spin twins' Laker and Lock destroyed Australia, taking 61 wickets between them, including Laker taking 19 wickets in the game (a first-class record) at Headingley, a game dubbed Laker's Match.

However, the team rebounded to win five consecutive series in the latter half of the 1950s, first under the leadership of Ian Johnson, then Ian Craig and Richie Benaud. The series against the West Indies in the 1960–61 season was notable for the Tied Test in the first game at the Gabba, which was the first in Test cricket. Australia ended up winning the series 2–1 after a hard-fought series that was praised for its excellent standards and sense of fair play. Stand-out players in that series as well as through the early part of the 1960s were Richie Benaud, who took a then-record number of wickets as a leg-spinner and who also captained Australia in 28 Tests, including 24 without defeat; Alan Davidson, who was a notable fast-bowler and also became the first player to take 10 wickets and make 100 runs in the same game in the first Test; Bob Simpson, who also later captained Australia for two different periods of time; Colin McDonald, the first-choice opening batsman for most of the 1950s and early '60s; Norm O'Neill, who made 181 in the Tied Test; Neil Harvey, towards the end of his long career; and Wally Grout, an excellent wicket-keeper who died at the age of 41.

- World Series Cricket and Restructuring

The Centenary Test was played in March 1977 at the MCG to celebrate 100 years since the first Test was played. Australia won the match by 45 runs, an identical result to the first Test match.

In May 1977, Kerry Packer announced he was organising a breakaway competition – World Series Cricket (WSC) – after the Australian Cricket Board (ACB) refused to accept Channel Nine's bid to gain exclusive television rights to Australia's Test matches in 1976. Packer secretly signed leading international cricketers to his competition, including 28 Australians. Almost all of the Australian Test team at the time were signed to WSC – notable exceptions including Gary Cosier, Geoff Dymock, Kim Hughes and Craig Serjeant – and the Australian selectors were forced to pick what was generally considered a third-rate team from players in the Sheffield Shield. Former player Bob Simpson, who had retired 10 years previously after a conflict with the board, was recalled at the age of 41 to captain Australia against India. Jeff Thomson was named deputy in a team that included seven debutants. Australia managed to win the series 3–2, mainly thanks to the batting of Simpson, who scored 539 runs, including two centuries; and the bowling of Wayne Clark, who took 28 wickets.

Australia lost the next series 3–1 against the West Indies, which was fielding a full strength team; and also lost the 1978–79 Ashes series 5–1, the team's worst Ashes result in Australia. Graham Yallop was named as captain for the Ashes, with Kim Hughes taking over for the 1979–80 tour of India. Rodney Hogg took 41 wickets in his debut series, an Australian record. WSC players returned to the team for the 1979–80 season after a settlement between the ACB and Kerry Packer. Greg Chappell was reinstated as captain.

The underarm bowling incident of 1981 occurred when, in an ODI against New Zealand, Greg Chappell instructed his brother Trevor to bowl an underarm delivery to New Zealand batsman Brian McKechnie, with New

Zealand needing a six to tie off the last ball. The aftermath of the incident soured political relations between Australia and New Zealand, with several leading political and cricketing figures calling it "unsportsmanlike" and "not in the spirit of cricket".

Australia continued its success up until the early 1980s, built around the Chappell brothers, Dennis Lillee, Jeff Thomson and Rod Marsh. The 1980s was a period of relative mediocrity after the turmoil caused by the Rebel Tours of South Africa and the subsequent retirement of several key players. The rebel tours were funded by the South African Cricket Board to compete against its national side, which had been banned—along with many other sports, including Olympic athletes—from competing internationally, due to the South African government's racist apartheid policies. Some of Australia's best players were poached: Graham Yallop, Carl Rackemann, Terry Alderman, Rodney Hogg, Kim Hughes, John Dyson, Greg Shipperd, Steve Rixon and Steve Smith amongst others. These players were handed three-year suspensions by the Australian Cricket Board which greatly weakened the player pool for the national sides, as most were either current representative players or on the verge of gaining honours.

- Australian cricket from 1985–86 to 2000

The so-called 'Golden Era' of Australian cricket occurred around the end of the 20th century and the beginning of the 21st century. This was a period in which Australian cricket recovered from the disruption caused by World Series Cricket to create arguably the strongest Test team in history.

Under the captaincy of Allan Border and the new fielding standards put in place by new coach Bob Simpson, the team was restructured and gradually rebuilt their cricketing stocks. Some of the rebel players returned to the national side after serving their suspensions, including Trevor Hohns, Carl Rackemann and Terry Alderman. During these lean years, it was the batsmen Border, David Boon, Dean Jones, the young Steve Waugh and the bowling feats of Alderman, Bruce Reid, Craig McDermott, Merv Hughes and to a lesser extent, Geoff Lawson who kept the Australian side afloat.

With the emergence of players such as Ian Healy, Mark Taylor, Geoff Marsh, Mark Waugh, and Greg Matthews in the late 1980s, Australia was on the way back from the doldrums. Winning the Ashes in 1989, the Australians got a roll on beating Pakistan, Sri Lanka and then followed it up with another Ashes win on home soil in 1991. The Australians went on to the West Indies and had their chances but ended up losing the series. However, they bounced back and beat the Indians in their next Test series. With the retirement of the champion but defensive, Allan Border, a new era of attacking cricket had begun under the leadership of firstly Mark Taylor and then Steve Waugh.

The 1990s and early 21st century were arguably Australia's most successful periods, unbeaten in all Ashes series played bar the famous 2005 series and achieving a hat-trick of World Cups. This success has been attributed to the restructuring of the team and system by Border, successive aggressive captains, and the effectiveness of several key players, most notably Glenn McGrath, Shane Warne, Justin Langer, Matthew Hayden, Steve Waugh, Adam Gilchrist, Michael Hussey and Ricky Ponting.

- Australian cricket from 2000–01

Following the 2006–07 Ashes series which Australia won 5 nil, Australia slipped in the rankings after the retirements of key players. In the 2013/14 Ashes series, Australia again defeated England 5 nil and climbed back to third in the ICC International Test rankings. In February/March 2014, Australia beat South Africa, the number 1 team in the world, 2–1 and overtook them to return to the top of the rankings. In 2015, Australia won the World Cup, losing just one game for the tournament.

As of December 2020, Australia are ranked first in the ICC Test Championship, fourth in the ICC ODI Championship and second in the ICC T20I Championship.

- 2018 Australian ball-tampering scandal

On 25 March 2018, during the third Test match against hosts South Africa; players Cameron Bancroft, Steve Smith, David Warner and the leadership group of the team were implicated in a ball tampering scandal. Smith and Bancroft admitted to conspiring to alter the condition of the ball by rubbing it with a piece of adhesive tape containing abrasive granules picked up from the ground (it was later revealed that sandpaper was used). Smith stated that the purpose was to gain an advantage by unlawfully changing the ball's surface in order to generate reverse swing.

Bancroft had been filmed tampering with the ball and after being informed he had been caught, he was seen to transfer a yellow object from a pocket to the inside front of his trousers to hide the evidence. Steve Smith and David Warner were stood down as captain and vice-captain during the third Test while head coach, Darren Lehmann was suspected to have assisted Cameron Bancroft to tamper the ball.

The ICC imposed a one-match ban and 100%-match-fee fine on Smith, while Bancroft was fined 75 per cent of his match fee and received 3 demerit points. Smith and Warner were both stripped of their captaincy roles by Cricket Australia and sent home from the tour (along with Bancroft). Tim Paine was appointed as captain for the fourth Test. Cricket Australia then suspended Smith and Warner from playing for 12 months and Bancroft for 9 months. Smith and Bancroft could not be considered for leadership roles for 12 months after the suspension, while Warner is banned from leadership of any Cricket Australia team for life.

In the aftermath of these events, Darren Lehmann announced his resignation as head coach at the end of the series with Justin Langer replacing him. On 8 May 2018, Tim Paine was also named as the ODI captain while Aaron Finch was reinstated as T20I captain hours later, although Finch replaced Paine as the ODI captain after the 5-0 ODI series whitewash in England in June 2018.

On 7 October 2018, Australia played their first Test match under new coach Justin Langer and a new leadership group, which included Tim Paine as Australia's 46th Test captain. After a 1–0 loss to Pakistan in a two match Test series against Pakistan in the UAE and a 2–1 defeat against India in a four match Test series, they found success against Sri Lanka, winning the two Test match series 2–0.

In 2019, Australia played in the Cricket World Cup, where they finished second in the group stage before being knocked out by England at Edgbaston in the semi-final. Australia went on to retain the Ashes during the 2019 Ashes series, the first time on English soil since 2001, by winning the fourth Test at Old Trafford.

In 2020–21, Australia hosted India for 3 ODIs, 3 T20Is, and 4 Tests. They won the ODI series 2–1, but lost the T20I series 2–1. Then, the two teams competed for the Border-Gavaskar Trophy which saw one of the greatest overseas Test triumphs by India in the 4th Test to win the series 2–1 with the 3rd Test being drawn.

- Team colours

For Test matches, the team wears Cricket Whites, with an optional sweater or sweater-vest with a green and gold V-neck for use in cold weather. The sponsor's (currently Alinta for home matches and Qantas for away matches) logo is displayed on the right side of the chest while the Cricket Australia emblem is displayed on the left. If the sweater is being worn the Cricket Australia emblem is displayed under the V-neck and the sponsor's logo is again displayed on the right side of the chest. The baggy green, the Australian Test cricket cap, is considered an essential part of the cricketing uniform and as a symbol of the national team, with new players being presented with one upon their selection in the team. The cap and the helmet both prominently display the Australian cricketing coat-of-arms instead of the Cricket Australia emblem. At the end of 2011, ASICS was named the manufacturer of the whites and limited over uniforms from Adidas, with the ASICS logo being displayed on the shirt and pants. Players may choose any manufacturer for their other gear (bat, pads, shoes, gloves, etc.).

In One Day International (ODI) cricket and Twenty20 International cricket, the team wears uniforms usually coloured green and gold, the national colours of Australia. There has been a variety of different styles and layouts used in both forms of the limited-overs game, with coloured clothing (sometimes known as "pyjamas") being introduced for World Series Cricket in the late 1970s. The Alinta or Qantas logo is prominently displayed on the shirts and other gears. The current home ODI kit consists of green as the primary colour and gold as the secondary colour. The away kit is the opposite of the home kit with gold as the primary colour and green as the secondary colour. The home Twenty20 kit consists of black with the natural colours of Australia, green and gold strips. However, since Australia beat New Zealand at the MCG in the 2015 Cricket World Cup wearing the gold uniform, it has also become their primary colour, with the hats used being called 'floppy gold', formerly known as 'baggy gold', a limited-overs equivalent to a baggy green. Until the early 2000s and briefly in early 2020, in ODIs, Australia wore yellow helmets, before using green helmets as in test matches.

Former suppliers were Asics (1999), ISC (2000–2001), Fila (2002–2003) and Adidas (2004–2010) among others. Before Travelex, some of the former sponsors were Coca-Cola (1993–1998), Fly Emirates (1999) and Carlton & United Breweries (2000–2001).

- match records

- Team

1. Australia is the most successful Test team in cricketing history. It has won more than 350 Test matches at a rate of almost 47%. The next best performance is by South Africa at 37%.
2. Australia have been involved in the only two Tied Tests played. The first occurred in December 1960, against the West Indies in Brisbane.The second occurred in September 1986, against India in Madras (Chennai).
3. Australia's largest victory in a Test match came on 24 February 2002. Australia defeated South Africa by an innings and 360 runs in Johannesburg.
4. Australia holds the record for the most consecutive wins with 16. This has been achieved twice; from October 1999 to February 2001 and from December 2005 to January 2008.
5. Australia shares the record for the most consecutive series victories winning 9 series from October 2005 to June 2008. This record is shared with England.
6. Australia's highest total in a Test match innings was recorded in Kingston, Jamaica against the West Indies in June 1955. Australia posted 758/8 in their first innings, with five players scoring a century.
7. Australia's lowest total in a Test match innings was recorded in Birmingham against England in May 1902. Australia were bowled all out for 36.
8. Australia are the only team to have lost a Test match after enforcing the follow-on, having been the losing side in all three such matches
9. The first Test in the 1894–95 Ashes.
10. The third Test of the 1981 Ashes.
11. The second Test in the 2000–01 Border-Gavaskar Trophy series against India.
12. Against India in March 2013, Australia became the first team in Test history to declare in their first innings and then lose by an innings.
13. In the 2013–14 Ashes series, Australia took all 100 wickets on offer in the 5–0 sweep over England.
14. Ricky Ponting and Steve Waugh have played in the most Test matches for Australia, both playing in 168 matches.

- Batting

1. Charles Bannerman faced the first ball in Test cricket, scored the first runs in Test cricket and also scored the first Test century.
2. Charles Bannerman also scored 67.34% of the Australian first innings total in match 1. This record remains to this day as the highest percentage of a completed innings total that has been scored by a single batsman.
3. Ricky Ponting has scored the most runs for Australia in Test cricket with 13,378 runs. Allan Border is second with 11,174 runs in 265 innings a record which was broken by Brian Lara during his innings of 226 against Australia while Steve Waugh has 10,927 in 260 innings.Allan Border was the first Australian batsman to pass 10,000 and the first ever batsman to pass 11,000 Test runs.Ricky Ponting was the first Australian batsman to pass 12,000 and 13,000 Test runs.
4. Matthew Hayden holds the record for the most runs in a single innings by an Australian with 380 in the first Test against Zimbabwe in Perth in October 2003.
5. Donald Bradman holds the record for the highest average by an Australian (or any other) cricketer of 99.94 runs per dismissal. Bradman played 52 Tests, scoring 29 centuries and a further 13 fifties.
6. Ricky Ponting holds the record for the most centuries by an Australian cricketer with 41. Former Australian captain Steve Waugh is in second position with 32 centuries from 260 innings.
7. Allan Border holds the record for the most fifties by an Australian cricketer with 63 in 265 innings.
8. Adam Gilchrist holds the record for the fastest century by an Australian.
9. Glenn McGrath holds the record for the most ducks by an Australian cricketer with 35 in 138 innings.

- Bowling

1. Billy Midwinter picked up the first five-wicket haul in a Test innings in match 1.
2. Fred Spofforth performed Test cricket's first hat-trick by dismissing Vernon Royle, Francis McKinnon and Tom Emmett in successive balls.
3. Fred Spofforth also took the first 10-wicket match haul in Test cricket.

4. Shane Warne holds the record for the most wickets by an Australian cricketer with 708 wickets in 145 Test matches.
5. Arthur Mailey holds the record for the best bowling figures in an innings by an Australian cricketer with 9/121 against England in February 1921.
6. Bob Massie holds the record for the best bowling figures in a match by an Australian cricketer with 16/137 against England in June 1972. That was also his first Test match for Australia.
7. J. J. Ferris holds the record for the best bowling average by an Australian bowler, taking 61 wickets at 12.70 in his career.
8. Clarrie Grimmett holds the record for the most wickets in a Test series with 44 against South Africa in 1935–36.

- Fielding and wicketkeeping

1. Ricky Ponting holds the record for the most catches in a career by an Australian fielder with 196 in 168 matches.
2. Jack Blackham performed the first stumping in Test cricket in match 1.
3. Adam Gilchrist holds the record for the most dismissals in a career by an Australian wicketkeeper with 416 in 96 matches.

- Team

1. Australia's highest total in a One-Day International innings is 434/4, scored off 50 overs against South Africa in Johannesburg on 12 March 2006. This was a world record score before the South Africans later surpassed it in the same match.
2. Australia's lowest total in a One-Day International innings is 70. This score has occurred twice; once against England in 1977 and once against New Zealand in 1986.
3. Australia's largest victory in One-Day International cricket is 275 runs. This occurred against Afghanistan at the 2015 World Cup in Australia.
4. Australia are the only team in the history of the World Cup to win 3 consecutive tournaments; 1999, 2003 and 2007.
5. Australia went undefeated at the World Cup for a record 34 consecutive matches. After being defeated by Pakistan in 1999, Australia would remain unbeaten until they were again defeated by Pakistan in 2011.
6. Australia have won the most World Cups – 5.

CHAPTER THREE

Australian Cricket history

- Australian Cricket history

Australian Cricket has a history spanning over 200 years. The earliest reports of the sport in Australia appeared in the Sydney Gazette - the first newspaper printed in the country in 1804 - and by 1826 there were records of clubs being formed in Sydney.

By 1832, clubs were forming in Tasmania; known at the time as Van Diemen's Land. In Western Australia, there is a record of labourers and mechanics taking on the builders of the new Government House as far back as 1835. The Melbourne Cricket Club was formed in 1838, and South Australia was participating in club cricket by 1839. From east to west, the sport was beginning to animate all corners of the nation.

In 1851, Victorians travelled to Tasmania to play the first intercolonial match, with 15,000 spectators in attendance. Such matches were known as Intercolonial matches until Federation in 1901, when they became Interstate matches.

1. The burgeoning sport required administration, with Boards of Control formed in New South Wales in 1857, Victoria in 1864 and South Australia in 1871.
2. There were tours of Australia by English sides in the summers of 1861/62 and 1863/64 before a team of Indigenous Australians became the first side to make a reciprocal tour to the northern hemisphere in the summer of 1868. That tour was led by Charles Lawrence, an Englishman who was part of the 1861/62 tour to Australia. He liked the country so much, he decided to stay.

3. Another English side – including the most famous player of the era, Dr W G Grace – toured Australia in 1873/74 before, in 1876/77, a combined New South Wales and Victorian side took on a touring English team at the Melbourne Cricket Ground for what became recognised as the first Test match. The Australians won by 45 runs and the match included an innings of 165 "not out" by the home side's Charles Bannerman, the first individual three-figure score in Test history.
4. An Australian side toured England in 1878 but the first Test match there did not occur until 1880 when the two sides met at The Oval in London. In 1882, after Australia's first victory on English soil, the legend of The Ashes – the mythical trophy that the two countries compete for in Test match cricket – began.
5. The Sheffield Shield domestic competition in Australia was initiated in 1892 by the Australasian Cricket Council, the first attempt at a national governing body. The Shield was the result of a donation by Lord Sheffield, the financier of an England tour of Australia in 1891/92.

As for the Council, it featured representatives of New South Wales, Victoria and South Australia with the aim of regulating Intercolonial cricket and organising international tours.

That latter role was one the players resisted, as private tours were a means for them to earn a living by playing the game. Indeed, in 1912, six of Australia's leading players - Warwick Armstrong, Vernon Ransford, Victor Trumper, Tibby Cotter, Hanson Carter and Clem Hill - all declined to tour England for a triangular tournament that also involved South Africa.

The public motive for their disquiet was that their choice of team manager had been rejected by the Australian Board of Control for International Cricket – the body formed in 1905 to replace the Australasian Cricket Council, which had been disbanded in 1899. But the underlying reason was the question of who should have access to the funds raised by such tours.

The trip took place without what became known as "The Big Six" and the control of the game by administrators over players became established. Armstrong would later go on to captain Australia to its first-ever clean-sweep of an Ashes series, a 5-0 success against a war-ravaged England team in 1920/21. That victory was spearheaded by fast bowlers Jack Gregory and Ted McDonald, establishing another principle in cricket that was to stand the test of time – whichever side had the best pace bowlers was more likely to prevail.

- The Meeting

The first meeting of the Australian Board of Control for International Cricket featured two representatives from each of New South Wales and Victoria. For its second meeting one delegate from Queensland was permitted to attend, and in 1906, three representatives of New South Wales, South Australia and Victoria plus one Queenslander were present. Tasmania's first delegate attended in 1907 and six years later they were joined by a single Western Australia official.

In 1914 and 1974 respectively, Queensland and Western Australia increased their representation to two delegates. By 1973, the body had become the Australian Cricket Board. It stayed that way until 2003, when the game's national governing body became Cricket Australia.

- The Sheffield Shield

The Sheffield Shield was played between three states – New South Wales, South Australia and Victoria – from its inception in 1892 until 1926/27, when Queensland joined. Western Australia was admitted in 1947/48 and Tasmania became the sixth state to play in the competition in 1977/78. Matches were timeless up to 1926/27, before becoming four-day contests. From 1982/83 the top two sides in the competition each season have played off in a final.

The first domestic one-day competition took place in the summer of 1969/70, although New Zealand competed until 1974/75, claiming victory three times. The Australian Capital Territory (ACT) had a side compete for three seasons from 1997/98.

- domestic Twenty20 tournament

A domestic Twenty20 tournament started in 2005/06. For its first six seasons, the competition was state-based before it was replaced by the Big Bash League in 2011/12 featuring eight teams; two each from New South Wales and Victoria plus one from Adelaide, Perth, Brisbane and Hobart. Unlike several other Twenty20 competitions around the world, Cricket Australia - as the governing body - retained overall control of the teams.

- *Women Cricket After Progress*

The history of women in cricket can be traced back to 1894, when a Tasmanian created the first local women's competition in Australia's history books. In 1931, the Australian Women's Cricket Association would form, with the Australian women's team taking to the world stage against England in 1934 in the first ever Test match. From Ruby Monaghan to Ellyse Perry. From grassroots to elite. This is the evolution of women's cricket in Australia.

Women's cricket in Australia is believed to have started in 1894 when a Tasmanian, Lily Poulett-Harris, created a local competition. Just over a decade later, in 1905, the Victorian Women's Cricket Association was formed, followed by the Australian Women's Cricket Association in 1931.

During the summer of 1930/31, the first Australian Women's National Cricket Championships (WNCC) took place. Three years, later women's international cricket was born when the Australian Women's Cricket Council invited the Women's Cricket Association of England to send a team on tour. That trip featured 14 three-day matches and included the first-ever Women's Test match.

From 1972/73, Australian domestic teams have taken part in the WNCC and play for the Ruth Preddey Cup, named after the former New South Wales player and journalist who helped to organize finance for a tour of England herself. A women's Twenty20 Cup was first played at national level in 2008/09, although the Australian Capital Territory and Tasmania were not admitted until the following summer.

The governing body for the women's game then merged with Cricket Australia in 2003, ensuring that the men's and women's sport was run by one single and unified body. That body formed the Women's Big Bash League; a domestic Twenty20 competition featuring the same sides as the men's short-form tournament in 2015.

- Today Women Cricket

In 2018, a record breaking 1,558,821 Australians actively engaged in cricket competitions or programs across the nation; an increase on nine per cent from the previous year. Six in every 10 new participants were females, and multicultural participation rose by four per cent, making up 22 per cent of all participants. Indigenous participation is also on the rise, with an increased participation level of one per cent.

CHAPTER FOUR

Cricket Knowledge

- Cricket Knowledge

Cricket is a bat-and-ball game played between two teams of eleven players on a field at the centre of which is a 22-yard (20-metre) pitch with a wicket at each end, each comprising two bails balanced on three stumps. The game proceeds when a player on the fielding team, called the bowler, "bowls" (propels) the ball from one end of the pitch towards the wicket at the other end. The batting side's players score runs by striking the bowled ball with a bat and running between the wickets, while the bowling side tries to prevent this by keeping the ball within the field and getting it to either wicket, and dismiss each batter (so they are "out"). Means of dismissal include being bowled, when the ball hits the stumps and dislodges the bails, and by the fielding side either catching a hit ball before it touches the ground, or hitting a wicket with the ball before a batter can cross the crease line in front of the wicket to complete a run. When ten batters have been dismissed, the innings ends and the teams swap roles. The game is adjudicated by two umpires, aided by a third umpire and match referee in international matches.

Forms of cricket range from Twenty20, with each team batting for a single innings of 20 overs and the game generally lasting three hours, to Test matches played over five days. Traditionally cricketers play in all-white kit, but in limited overs cricket they wear club or team colours. In addition to the basic kit, some players wear protective gear to prevent injury caused by the ball, which is a hard, solid spheroid made of compressed leather with a slightly raised sewn seam enclosing a cork core layered with tightly wound string.

The earliest reference to cricket is in South East England in the mid-16th century. It spread globally with the expansion of the British Empire, with the first international matches in the second half of the 19th century. The game's governing body is the International Cricket Council (ICC), which has over 100 members, twelve of which are full members who play Test matches. The game's rules, the Laws of Cricket, are maintained by Marylebone Cricket Club (MCC) in London. The sport is followed primarily in South Asia, Australasia, the United Kingdom, southern Africa and the West Indies.Women's cricket, which is organised and played separately, has also achieved international standard. The most successful side playing international cricket is Australia, which has won seven One Day International trophies, including five World Cups, more than any other country and has been the top-rated Test side more than any other country.

- History of cricket to 1725

A medieval "club ball" game involving an underhand bowl towards a batter. Ball catchers are shown positioning themselves to catch a ball. Detail from the Canticles of Holy Mary, 13th century.

Cricket is one of many games in the "club ball" sphere that basically involve hitting a ball with a hand-held implement; others include baseball (which shares many similarities with cricket, both belonging in the more specific bat-and-ball games category), golf, hockey, tennis, squash, badminton and table tennis. In cricket's case, a key difference is the existence of a solid target structure, the wicket (originally, it is thought, a "wicket gate" through which sheep were herded), that the batter must defend. The cricket historian Harry Altham identified three "groups" of "club ball" games: the "hockey group", in which the ball is driven to and fro between two targets (the goals); the "golf group", in which the ball is driven towards an undefended target (the hole); and the "cricket group", in which "the ball is aimed at a mark (the wicket) and driven away from it".

It is generally believed that cricket originated as a children's game in the south-eastern counties of England, sometime during the medieval period.Although there are claims for prior dates, the earliest definite reference to cricket being played comes from evidence given at a court case in Guildford in January 1597 (Old Style), equating to January 1598 in the modern calendar. The case concerned ownership of a certain plot of land and the court heard the testimony of a 59-year-old coroner, John Derrick, who gave witness that.

Being a scholler in the ffree schoole of Guldeford hee and diverse of his fellows did runne and play there at creckett and other plaies.

Given Derrick's age, it was about half a century earlier when he was at school and so it is certain that cricket was being played c. 1550 by boys in Surrey. The view that it was originally a children's game is reinforced by Randle Cotgrave's 1611 English-French dictionary in which he defined the noun "crosse" as "the crooked staff wherewith boys play at cricket" and the verb form "crosser" as "to play at cricket".

One possible source for the sport's name is the Old English word "cryce" (or "cricc") meaning a crutch or staff. In Samuel Johnson's Dictionary, he derived cricket from "cryce, Saxon, a stick". In Old French, the word "criquet" seems to have meant a kind of club or stick. Given the strong medieval trade connections between south-east England and the County of Flanders when the latter belonged to the Duchy of Burgundy, the name may have been derived from the Middle Dutch (in use in Flanders at the time) "krick"(-e), meaning a stick (crook). Another possible source is the Middle Dutch word "krickstoel", meaning a long low stool used for kneeling in church and which resembled the long low wicket with two stumps used in early cricket. According to Heiner Gillmeister, a European language expert of Bonn University, "cricket" derives from the Middle Dutch phrase for hockey, met de (krik ket)sen (i.e., "with the stick chase"). Gillmeister has suggested that not only the name but also the sport itself may be of Flemish origin.

- Growth of amateur and professional cricket in England

Evolution of the cricket bat. The original "hockey stick" (left) evolved into the straight bat from c. 1760 when pitched delivery bowling began.

Although the main object of the game has always been to score the most runs, the early form of cricket differed from the modern game in certain key technical aspects; the North American variant of cricket known as wicket retained many of these aspects. The ball was bowled underarm by the bowler and along the ground towards a batter armed with a bat that in shape resembled a hockey stick; the batter defended a low, two-stump wicket; and runs were called notches because the scorers recorded them by notching tally sticks.

In 1611, the year Cotgrave's dictionary was published, ecclesiastical court records at Sidlesham in Sussex state that two parishioners, Bartholomew Wyatt and Richard Latter, failed to attend church on Easter Sunday because they were playing cricket. They were fined 12d each and ordered to do penance.This is the earliest mention of adult participation in cricket and it was around the same time that the earliest known organised inter-parish or village match was played – at Chevening, Kent. In 1624, a player called Jasper Vinall died after he was accidentally struck on the head during a match between two parish teams in Sussex.

Cricket remained a low-key local pursuit for much of the 17th century. It is known, through numerous references found in the records of ecclesiastical court cases, to have been proscribed at times by the Puritans before and during the Commonwealth. The problem was nearly always the issue of Sunday play as the Puritans considered cricket to be "profane" if played on the Sabbath, especially if large crowds or gambling were involved.

According to the social historian Derek Birley, there was a "great upsurge of sport after the Restoration" in 1660. Gambling on sport became a problem significant enough for Parliament to pass the 1664 Gambling Act, limiting stakes to £100 which was, in any case, a colossal sum exceeding the annual income of 99% of the population. Along with prizefighting, horse racing and blood sports, cricket was perceived to be a gambling sport.Rich patrons made matches for high stakes, forming teams in which they engaged the first professional players.By the end of the century, cricket had developed into a major sport that was spreading throughout England and was already being taken abroad by English mariners and colonisers – the earliest reference to cricket overseas is dated 1676. A 1697 newspaper report survives of "a great cricket match" played in Sussex "for fifty guineas apiece" – this is the earliest known contest that is generally considered a First Class match.

- The patrons, and other players from the social class known as the "gentry", began to classify themselves as "amateurs" to establish a clear distinction from the professionals, who were invariably members of the working class, even to the point of having separate changing and dining facilities. The gentry, including such high-ranking nobles as the Dukes of Richmond, exerted their honour code of noblesse oblige to claim rights of leadership in any sporting contests they took part in, especially as it was necessary for them to play alongside their "social inferiors" if they were to win their bets. In time, a perception took hold that the typical amateur who played in first-class cricket, until 1962 when amateurism was abolished, was someone with a public school education who had then gone to one of Cambridge or Oxford University – society insisted that such people were "officers and gentlemen" whose destiny was to provide leadership. In a purely financial sense, the cricketing amateur would theoretically claim expenses for playing while his professional counterpart played under contract and was paid a wage or match fee; in practice, many amateurs claimed more than actual expenditure and the derisive term "shamateur" was coined to describe the practice.

- The Young Cricketer, 1768

The game underwent major development in the 18th century to become England's national sport.Its success was underwritten by the twin necessities of patronage and betting. Cricket was prominent in London as early as 1707 and, in the middle years of the century, large crowds flocked to matches on the Artillery Ground in Finsbury. The single wicket form of the sport attracted huge crowds and wagers to match, its popularity peaking in the 1748 season. Bowling underwent an evolution around 1760 when bowlers began to pitch the ball instead of rolling or skimming it towards the batter. This caused a revolution in bat design because, to deal with the bouncing ball, it was necessary to introduce the modern straight bat in place of the old "hockey stick" shape.

The Hambledon Club was founded in the 1760s and, for the next twenty years until the formation of Marylebone Cricket Club (MCC) and the opening of Lord's Old Ground in 1787, Hambledon was both the game's greatest club and its focal point. MCC quickly became the sport's premier club and the custodian of the Laws of Cricket. New Laws introduced in the latter part of the 18th century included the three stump wicket and leg before wicket (lbw).

The 19th century saw underarm bowling superseded by first roundarm and then overarm bowling. Both developments were controversial.Organisation of the game at county level led to the creation of the county clubs, starting with Sussex in 1839. In December 1889, the eight leading county clubs formed the official County Championship, which began in 1890.

The most famous player of the 19th century was W. G. Grace, who started his long and influential career in 1865. It was especially during the career of Grace that the distinction between amateurs and professionals became blurred by the existence of players like him who were nominally amateur but, in terms of their financial gain, de facto professional. Grace himself was said to have been paid more money for playing cricket than any professional.

The last two decades before the First World War have been called the "Golden Age of cricket". It is a nostalgic name prompted by the collective sense of loss resulting from the war, but the period did produce some great players and memorable matches, especially as organised competition at county and Test level developed.

- Cricket becomes an international sport

In 1844, the first-ever international match took place between the United States and Canada. In 1859, a team of English players went to North America on the first overseas tour. Meanwhile, the British Empire had been instrumental in spreading the game overseas and by the middle of the 19th century it had become well established in Australia, the Caribbean, India, Pakistan, New Zealand, North America and South Africa.

In 1862, an English team made the first tour of Australia. The first Australian team to travel overseas consisted of Aboriginal stockmen who toured England in 1868. The first One Day International match was played on 5 January 1971 between Australia and England at the Melbourne Cricket Ground.

In 1876–77, an England team took part in what was retrospectively recognised as the first-ever Test match at the Melbourne Cricket Ground against Australia. The rivalry between England and Australia gave birth to The Ashes in 1882, and this has remained Test cricket's most famous contest. Test cricket began to expand in 1888–89 when South Africa played England.

- World cricket in the 20th century

The inter-war years were dominated by Australia's Don Bradman, statistically the greatest Test batter of all time. Test cricket continued to expand during the 20th century with the addition of the West Indies (1928),

New Zealand (1930) and India (1932) before the Second World War and then Pakistan (1952), Sri Lanka (1982), Zimbabwe (1992), Bangladesh (2000), Ireland and Afghanistan (both 2018) in the post-war period. South Africa was banned from international cricket from 1970 to 1992 as part of the apartheid boycott.

- The rise of limited overs cricket

Cricket entered a new era in 1963 when English counties introduced the limited overs variant. As it was sure to produce a result, limited overs cricket was lucrative and the number of matches increased. The first Limited Overs International was played in 1971 and the governing International Cricket Council (ICC), seeing its potential, staged the first limited overs Cricket World Cup in 1975. In the 21st century, a new limited overs form, Twenty20, made an immediate impact. On 22 June 2017, Afghanistan and Ireland became the 11th and 12th ICC full members, enabling them to play Test cricket.

- A typical cricket field.

In cricket, the rules of the game are specified in a code called The Laws of Cricket (hereinafter called "the Laws") which has a global remit. There are 42 Laws (always written with a capital "L"). The earliest known version of the code was drafted in 1744 and, since 1788, it has been owned and maintained by its custodian, the Marylebone Cricket Club (MCC) in London.

- Playing area

Cricket is a bat-and-ball game played on a cricket field between two teams of eleven players each. The field is usually circular or oval in shape and the edge of the playing area is marked by a boundary, which may be a fence, part of the stands, a rope, a painted line or a combination of these; the boundary must if possible be marked along its entire length.

In the approximate centre of the field is a rectangular pitch (see image, below) on which a wooden target called a wicket is sited at each end; the wickets are placed 22 yards (20 m) apart. The pitch is a flat surface 10 feet (3.0 m) wide, with very short grass that tends to be worn away as the game progresses (cricket can also be played on artificial surfaces, notably matting). Each wicket is made of three wooden stumps topped by two bails.

- Cricket pitch and creases

As illustrated above, the pitch is marked at each end with four white painted lines: a bowling crease, a popping crease and two return creases. The three stumps are aligned centrally on the bowling crease, which is eight feet eight inches long. The popping crease is drawn four feet in front of the bowling crease and parallel to it; although it is drawn as a twelve-foot line (six feet either side of the wicket), it is, in fact, unlimited in length. The return creases are drawn at right angles to the popping crease so that they intersect the ends of the bowling crease; each return crease is drawn as an eight-foot line, so that it extends four feet behind the bowling crease, but is also, in fact, unlimited in length.

Before a match begins, the team captains (who are also players) toss a coin to decide which team will bat first and so take the first innings. Innings is the term used for each phase of play in the match.In each innings, one team bats, attempting to score runs, while the other team bowls and fields the ball, attempting to restrict the scoring and dismiss the batters. When the first innings ends, the teams change roles; there can be two to four innings depending upon the type of match. A match with four scheduled innings is played over three to five days; a match with two scheduled innings is usually completed in a single day. During an innings, all eleven members of the fielding team take the field, but usually only two members of the batting team are on the field at any given time. The exception to this is if a batter has any type of illness or injury restricting his or her ability to run, in this case the batter is allowed a runner who can run between the wickets when the batter hits a scoring run or runs,though this does not apply in international cricket. The order of batters is usually announced just before the match, but it can be varied.

The main objective of each team is to score more runs than their opponents but, in some forms of cricket, it is also necessary to dismiss all of the opposition batters in their final innings in order to win the match, which would otherwise be drawn. If the team batting last is all out having scored fewer runs than their opponents, they are said to have "lost by n runs" (where n is the difference between the aggregate number of runs scored by the teams). If the team that bats last scores enough runs to win, it is said to have "won by n wickets", where n is the number of wickets left to fall. For example, a team that passes its opponents' total having lost six wickets (i.e., six of their batters have been dismissed) have won the match "by four wickets".

In a two-innings-a-side match, one team's combined first and second innings total may be less than the other side's first innings total. The team with the greater score is then said to have "won by an innings and n runs", and does not need to bat again: n is the difference between the two teams' aggregate scores. If the team batting last is all out, and both sides have scored the same number of runs, then the match is a tie; this result is quite rare in matches of two innings a side with only 62 happening in first-class matches from the earliest known instance in 1741 until January 2017. In the traditional form of the game, if the time allotted for the match expires before either side can win, then the game is declared a draw.

If the match has only a single innings per side, then a maximum number of overs applies to each innings. Such a match is called a "limited overs" or "one-day" match, and the side scoring more runs wins regardless of the number of wickets lost, so that a draw cannot occur. In some cases, ties are broken by having each team bat for a one-over innings known as a Super Over; subsequent Super Overs may be played if the first Super Over ends in a tie. If this kind of match is temporarily interrupted by bad weather, then a complex mathematical formula, known as the Duckworth–Lewis–Stern method after its developers, is often used to recalculate a new target score. A one-day match can also be declared a "no-result" if fewer than a previously agreed number of overs have been bowled by either team, in circumstances that make normal resumption of play impossible; for example, wet weather.

In all forms of cricket, the umpires can abandon the match if bad light or rain makes it impossible to continue. There have been instances of entire matches, even Test matches scheduled to be played over five days, being lost to bad weather without a ball being bowled: for example, the third Test of the 1970/71 series in Australia.

- Innings

The innings (ending with 's' in both singular and plural form) is the term used for each phase of play during a match. Depending on the type of match being played, each team has either one or two innings. Sometimes all eleven members of the batting side take a turn to bat but, for various reasons, an innings can end before they have all done so. The innings terminates if the batting team is "all out", a term defined by the Laws: "at the fall of a wicket or the retirement of a batter, further balls remain to be bowled but no further batter is available to come in". In this situation, one of the batters has not been dismissed and is termed not out; this is because he has no partners left and there must always be two active batters while the innings is in progress.

- An innings may end early while there are still two not out batters

the batting team's captain may declare the innings closed even though some of his players have not had a turn to bat: this is a tactical decision by the captain, usually because he believes his team have scored sufficient runs and need time to dismiss the opposition in their innings

the set number of overs (i.e., in a limited overs match) have been bowled

the match has ended prematurely due to bad weather or running out of time

in the final innings of the match, the batting side has reached its target and won the game.

- Overs

The Laws state that, throughout an innings, "the ball shall be bowled from each end alternately in overs of 6 balls". The name "over" came about because the umpire calls "Over!" when six balls have been bowled. At this point, another bowler is deployed at the other end, and the fielding side changes ends while the batters do not. A bowler cannot bowl two successive overs, although a bowler can (and usually does) bowl alternate overs, from the same end, for several overs which are termed a "spell". The batters do not change ends at the end of the over, and so the one who was non-striker is now the striker and vice versa. The umpires also change positions so that the one who was at "square leg" now stands behind the wicket at the non-striker's end and vice versa.

- Clothing and equipment

English cricketer W. G. Grace "taking guard" in 1883. His pads and bat are very similar to those used today. The gloves have evolved somewhat. Many modern players use more defensive equipment than were available to Grace, most notably helmets and arm guards.

The wicket-keeper (a specialised fielder behind the batter) and the batters wear protective gear because of the hardness of the ball, which can be delivered at speeds of more than 145 kilometres per hour (90 mph) and presents a major health and safety concern. Protective clothing includes pads (designed to protect the knees and shins), batting gloves or wicket-keeper's gloves for the hands, a safety helmet for the head and a box for male players inside the trousers (to protect the crotch area). Some batters wear additional padding inside their shirts and trousers such as thigh pads, arm pads, rib protectors and shoulder pads. The only fielders allowed to wear protective gear are those in positions very close to the batter (i.e., if they are alongside or in front of him), but they cannot wear gloves or external leg guards.

Subject to certain variations, on-field clothing generally includes a collared shirt with short or long sleeves; long trousers; woolen pullover (if needed); cricket cap (for fielding) or a safety helmet; and spiked shoes or boots to increase traction. The kit is traditionally all white and this remains the case in Test and first-class cricket but, in limited overs cricket, team colours are worn instead.

- Bat and ball

Two types of cricket ball, both of the same size:

i) A used white ball. White balls are mainly used in limited overs cricket, especially in matches played at night, under floodlights (left).

ii) A used red ball. Red balls are used in Test cricket, first-class cricket and some other forms of cricket (right).

The essence of the sport is that a bowler delivers (i.e., bowls) the ball from his or her end of the pitch towards the batter who, armed with a bat, is "on strike" at the other end (see next sub-section: Basic gameplay).

The bat is made of wood, usually Salix alba (white willow), and has the shape of a blade topped by a cylindrical handle. The blade must not be more than 4.25 inches (10.8 cm) wide and the total length of the bat not more than 38 inches (97 cm). There is no standard for the weight, which is usually between 2 lb 7 oz and 3 lb (1.1 and 1.4 kg).

The ball is a hard leather-seamed spheroid, with a circumference of 9 inches (23 cm). The ball has a "seam": six rows of stitches attaching the leather shell of the ball to the string and cork interior. The seam on a new ball is prominent and helps the bowler propel it in a less predictable manner. During matches, the quality of the ball deteriorates to a point where it is no longer usable; during the course of this deterioration, its behaviour in flight will change and can influence the outcome of the match. Players will, therefore, attempt to modify the ball's behaviour by modifying its physical properties. Polishing the ball and wetting it with sweat or saliva is legal, even when the polishing is deliberately done on one side only to increase the ball's swing through the air, but the acts of rubbing other substances into the ball, scratching the surface or picking at the seam are illegal ball tampering.

- Player roles

Basic gameplay: bowler to batter

During normal play, thirteen players and two umpires are on the field. Two of the players are batters and the rest are all eleven members of the fielding team. The other nine players in the batting team are off the field in the pavilion. The image with overlay below shows what is happening when a ball is being bowled and which of the personnel are on or close to the pitch.

- Return crease

In the photo, the two batters (3 & 8; wearing yellow) have taken position at each end of the pitch (6). Three members of the fielding team (4, 10 & 11; wearing dark blue) are in shot. One of the two umpires (1; wearing white hat) is stationed behind the wicket (2) at the bowler's (4) end of the pitch. The bowler (4) is bowling the ball (5) from his end of the pitch to the batter at the other end who is called the "striker". The other batter (3) at the bowling end is called the "non-striker". The wicket-keeper (10), who is a specialist, is positioned behind the striker's wicket (9) and behind him stands one of the fielders in a position called "first slip" (11). While the bowler and the first slip are wearing conventional kit only, the two batters and the wicket-keeper are wearing protective gear including safety helmets, padded gloves and leg guards (pads).

While the umpire (1) in shot stands at the bowler's end of the pitch, his colleague stands in the outfield, usually in or near the fielding position called "square leg", so that he is in line with the popping crease (7) at the striker's end of the pitch. The bowling crease (not numbered) is the one on which the wicket is located between the return creases (12). The bowler (4) intends to hit the wicket (9) with the ball (5) or, at least, to prevent the striker (8) from scoring runs. The striker (8) intends, by using his bat, to defend his wicket and, if possible, to hit the ball away from the pitch in order to score runs.

Some players are skilled in both batting and bowling, or as either or these as well as wicket-keeping, so are termed all-rounders. Bowlers are classified according to their style, generally as fast bowlers, seam bowlers or spinners. Batters are classified according to whether they are right-handed or left-handed.

- Fielding

Of the eleven fielders, three are in shot in the image above. The other eight are elsewhere on the field, their positions determined on a tactical basis by the captain or the bowler. Fielders often change position between deliveries, again as directed by the captain or bowler.

If a fielder is injured or becomes ill during a match, a substitute is allowed to field instead of him, but the substitute cannot bowl or act as a captain, except in the case of concussion substitutes in international cricket. The substitute leaves the field when the injured player is fit to return. The Laws of Cricket were updated in 2017 to allow substitutes to act as wicket-keepers.

- Bowling and dismissal

Glenn McGrath of Australia holds the world record for most wickets in the Cricket World Cup.

Most bowlers are considered specialists in that they are selected for the team because of their skill as a bowler, although some are all-rounders and even specialist batters bowl occasionally. The specialists bowl several times during an innings but may not bowl two overs consecutively. If the captain wants a bowler to "change ends", another bowler must temporarily fill in so that the change is not immediate.

A bowler reaches his delivery stride by means of a "run-up" and an over is deemed to have begun when the bowler starts his run-up for the first delivery of that over, the ball then being "in play".

Fast bowlers, needing momentum, take a lengthy run up while bowlers with a slow delivery take no more than a couple of steps before bowling. The fastest bowlers can deliver the ball at a speed of over 145 kilometres per hour (90 mph) and they sometimes rely on sheer speed to try to defeat the batter, who is forced to react very quickly.

Other fast bowlers rely on a mixture of speed and guile by making the ball seam or swing (i.e. curve) in flight. This type of delivery can deceive a batter into miscuing his shot, for example, so that the ball just touches the edge of the bat and can then be "caught behind" by the wicket-keeper or a slip fielder. At the other end of the bowling scale is the spin bowler who bowls at a relatively slow pace and relies entirely on guile to deceive the batter. A spinner will often "buy his wicket" by "tossing one up" (in a slower, steeper parabolic path) to lure the batter into making a poor shot. The batter has to be very wary of such deliveries as they are often "flighted" or spun so that the ball will not behave quite as he expects and he could be "trapped" into getting himself out. In between the pacemen and the spinners are the medium paced seamers who rely on persistent accuracy to try to contain the rate of scoring and wear down the batter's concentration.

There are nine ways in which a batter can be dismissed: five relatively common and four extremely rare. The common forms of dismissal are bowled, caught, leg before wicket (lbw), run out and stumped. Rare methods are hit wicket,hit the ball twice, obstructing the field and timed out. The Laws state that the fielding team, usually the bowler in practice, must appeal for a dismissal before the umpire can give his decision. If the batter is out, the umpire raises a forefinger and says "Out!"; otherwise, he will shake his head and say "Not out".There is, effectively, a tenth method of dismissal, retired out, which is not an on-field dismissal as such but rather a retrospective one for which no fielder is credited.

- Batting, runs and extras

The directions in which a right-handed batter, facing down the page, intends to send the ball when playing various cricketing shots. The diagram for a left-handed batter is a mirror image of this one.

Batters take turns to bat via a batting order which is decided beforehand by the team captain and presented to the umpires, though the order remains flexible when the captain officially nominates the team. Substitute batters are generally not allowed, except in the case of concussion substitutes in international cricket.

In order to begin batting the batter first adopts a batting stance. Standardly, this involves adopting a slight crouch with the feet pointing across the front of the wicket, looking in the direction of the bowler, and holding the bat so it passes over the feet and so its tip can rest on the ground near to the toes of the back foot.

A skilled batter can use a wide array of "shots" or "strokes" in both defensive and attacking mode. The idea is to hit the ball to the best effect with the flat surface of the bat's blade. If the ball touches the side of the bat it is called an "edge". The batter does not have to play a shot and can allow the ball to go through to the wicketkeeper. Equally, he does not have to attempt a run when he hits the ball with his bat. Batters do not always seek to hit the ball as hard as possible, and a good player can score runs just by making a deft stroke with a turn of the wrists or by simply "blocking" the ball but directing it away from fielders so that he has time to take a run. A wide variety of shots are played, the batter's repertoire including strokes named according to the style of swing and the direction aimed: e.g., "cut", "drive", "hook", "pull".

The batter on strike (i.e. the "striker") must prevent the ball hitting the wicket, and try to score runs by hitting the ball with his bat so that he and his partner have time to run from one end of the pitch to the other before the fielding side can return the ball. To register a run, both runners must touch the ground behind the popping crease with either their bats or their bodies (the batters carry their bats as they run). Each completed run increments the score of both the team and the striker.

- Sachin Tendulkar is the only player to have scored one hundred international centuries

The decision to attempt a run is ideally made by the batter who has the better view of the ball's progress, and this is communicated by calling: usually "yes", "no" or "wait". More than one run can be scored from a single hit: hits worth one to three runs are common, but the size of the field is such that it is usually difficult to run four or more. To compensate for this, hits that reach the boundary of the field are automatically awarded four runs if the ball touches the ground en route to the boundary or six runs if the ball clears the boundary without touching the ground within the boundary. In these cases the batters do not need to run. Hits for five are unusual and generally rely on the help of "overthrows" by a fielder returning the ball. If an odd number of runs is scored by the striker, the two batters have changed ends, and the one who was non-striker is now the striker. Only the striker can score individual runs, but all runs are added to the team's total.

Additional runs can be gained by the batting team as extras (called "sundries" in Australia) due to errors made by the fielding side. This is achieved in four ways: no-ball, a penalty of one extra conceded by the bowler if he breaks the rules; wide, a penalty of one extra conceded by the bowler if he bowls so that the ball is out of the batter's reach bye, an extra awarded if the batter misses the ball and it goes past the wicket-keeper and gives the batters time to run in the conventional way leg bye, as for a bye except that the ball has hit the batter's body, though not his bat. If the bowler has conceded a no-ball or a wide, his team incurs an additional penalty because that ball (i.e., delivery) has to be bowled again and hence the batting side has the opportunity to score more runs from this extra ball.

- Specialist roles

Captain (cricket) and Wicket-keeper

The captain is often the most experienced player in the team, certainly the most tactically astute, and can possess any of the main skillsets as a batter, a bowler or a wicket-keeper. Within the Laws, the captain has certain responsibilities in terms of nominating his players to the umpires before the match and ensuring that his players conduct themselves "within the spirit and traditions of the game as well as within the Laws".

The wicket-keeper (sometimes called simply the "keeper") is a specialist fielder subject to various rules within the Laws about his equipment and demeanour. He is the only member of the fielding side who can effect a stumping and is the only one permitted to wear gloves and external leg guards. Depending on their primary skills, the other ten players in the team tend to be classified as specialist batters or specialist bowlers. Generally, a team will include five or six specialist batters and four or five specialist bowlers, plus the wicket-keeper.

- Umpires and scorers

Umpire (cricket), Scoring (cricket), and Cricket statistics

An umpire signals a decision to the scorers

The game on the field is regulated by the two umpires, one of whom stands behind the wicket at the bowler's end, the other in a position called "square leg" which is about 15–20 metres away from the batter on strike and in line with the popping crease on which he is taking guard. The umpires have several responsibilities including adjudication on whether a ball has been correctly bowled (i.e., not a no-ball or a wide); when a run is scored; whether a batter is out (the fielding side must first appeal to the umpire, usually with the phrase "How's that?" or "Owzat?"); when intervals start and end; and the suitability of the pitch, field and weather for playing the game. The umpires are authorised to interrupt or even abandon a match due to circumstances likely to endanger the players, such as a damp pitch or deterioration of the light.

Off the field in televised matches, there is usually a third umpire who can make decisions on certain incidents with the aid of video evidence. The third umpire is mandatory under the playing conditions for Test and Limited Overs International matches played between two ICC full member countries. These matches also have a match referee whose job is to ensure that play is within the Laws and the spirit of the game.

The match details, including runs and dismissals, are recorded by two official scorers, one representing each team. The scorers are directed by the hand signals of an umpire . For example, the umpire raises a forefinger to signal that the batter is out (has been dismissed); he raises both arms above his head if the batter has hit the ball for six runs. The scorers are required by the Laws to record all runs scored, wickets taken and overs bowled; in practice, they also note significant amounts of additional data relating to the game.

A match's statistics are summarised on a scorecard. Prior to the popularisation of scorecards, most scoring was done by men sitting on vantage points cuttings notches on tally sticks and runs were originally called notches.According to Rowland Bowen, the earliest known scorecard templates were introduced in 1776 by T. Pratt of Sevenoaks and soon came into general use.It is believed that scorecards were printed and sold at Lord's for the first time in 1846.

- thank you for buy & read this book

  have a great day of your
  from : Mr Vivek Kumar Pandey

- This All Credit Goes To My Super Hero Daddy. "Always Love You dad'.

Printed by Libri Plureos GmbH in Hamburg,
Germany